Flow Posing

The Practical Guide for Wedding Photographers

I0455296

Johnie L. Cook

Flow Posing

The Practical Guide for Wedding Photographers

Johnie L. Cook
Copyright 2012
CPP (Certified Professional Photographer) retired
With over 30 years' experience in wedding
photography

Published by
Econohost Publications
Econohost.info

3

PREFACE

Filling in for a photographer at a local aircraft company when he went to the hospital for surgery, I was asked if I would consider transferring into the photo lab full time, with a upgrade of two labor grades (higher wages) and the opportunity to do what I wanted to do anyway, take photographs.

That started a 25 year history with Beech Aircraft and unbelievable opportunities. I have photographed dignitaries, movie stars, astronauts, sports figures, advertising photographs, air to air photography and so much more.

One of my highest honors was to study, and test for, and earned that "Certified Professional Photographer" Degree from Professional Photographers of America. Not an easy task to accomplish. I continued with that honor until I retired.

My hopes in writing; **"Flow Posing"** is to help those out there to bring back some professionalism into the field. With the invention of the digital camera, it became pretty easy for anyone with a camera to call himself/herself a "professional".

But what I'm seeing being produced is a long way from what I know as "professional photography".

I have a plaque in my office right up front where the bride can see it that says:

"The Bitterness of Low Quality Lingers Long After the Sweetness of Low Price"

I hope this book will help you get to the point of being that "Professional Photographer".

Table of Contents

Chapter 1

The Practical Guide for Wedding Photographers

F irst things first, understand this isn't a book about "technical stuff", not about pixels, not about white balance, not about f-stops and shutter speeds and not much about equipment.

You should already know this stuff and be very familiar with your camera equipment before you ever take money to photograph a wedding. If you need help with composition and color try this guide http:// amazon.com/dp/B006QDBUF4. There are lots of good cameras and systems out there, pick and chose carefully and then learn your "choice". Practice with it someplace besides at a wedding!

Like they used to say in the Army "your gun is your friend and it can save your life". Well, "your camera is your friend and it can make you a lot of money" if you learn how to use it. Learn what pictures to take that your bride and groom can't live without!

Remember; if you are starting a new business from scratch or creating a business from a hobby, you will need to invest in the necessary equipment to make it happen.

All businesses must have a professional level of service; that is what separates the winners from the losers. I would suggest that as a wedding photographer you will need at least the following level of equipment to accomplish your job.

Chapter 2

Equipment Needed

These are a few, what I consider professional "**Must have**" items.

Get and use a **good steady tripod** for all your "time exposures", and when doing the formal groups. It is needed for the long exposures during ceremony and when doing the formal groups, so you can leave the camera mounted on the tripod, and then you don't have to pick it and put it down every time you need to physically move to the group to help arrange and/or put finishing touches on a pose. I used a Bogen 3021 (now a 055XPROB) http://goo.gl/3erZ8.

I am suggesting you purchase one like the "Special "updated Bogen 055XPROB system, it is a good sturdy tripod and not too heavy, it is never going to become a burden. It is also a great tripod for video with its ball quick release head.

If you shoot video you should invest in wireless microphones for both bride and groom (cheaper ones can be found at www.amazon.com), (since the bride and groom usually talk very low), using the microphones for recording could be a "very profitable service" for your billing strategy. Start with the basic microphone and if possible get good wireless microphones and place it on the groom, so that the bride, groom, and the pastor's voice can be picked up easily at the time of the vows.

I also use a "**Just Rite**" Digital PRO-M camera bracket that you can order online at http://goo.gl/3erZ8.

This "Made in America" bracket (can be found at www.amazon.com for online purchase) allows your flash unit to be mounted up above your camera, allowing the camera to be rotated for horizontal and vertical photos without the flash being mounted on the camera. By raising the flash unit up, it helps eliminate "**red eye**" and allows shadows to fall down behind your subject. It also comes with a "quick release" bracket that mounts to the tripod and the bottom of your camera that allows, just like the name "a quick release" of camera and bracket from the tripod".

Another nice feature of this bracket is that it has "feet" on the bottom of it that allows the camera to be set down without falling over, another handy feature when you're moving fast and need to use both hands, just set it down, make adjustments or move items when you need two hands and it's right there for you to easily pick up when you need it again, it's not cheap, but in my opinion one of the best for what you're wanting to do; be a wedding photographer".

Built solidly by a master craftsman and former photographer, Gary Justice', the "Just Rite" camera bracket does everything we want it to do.

About the equipment, remember to have backup equipment with you. If any of your equipment fails, these moments can never be captured again by any means, as they are unique events by themselves and one of the most memorable ones in life. There is no re-shoot if you mess up.

Cameras from Nikon and Canon has always been the "Top of the Line for professionals".

The "**Minimum**" camera for starting out your photography business; I recommend a Nikon D5100 SLR Digital camera w/ 16.2MP (you can get one online from http://goo.gl/MeoHT). This is an **inexpensive professional** camera and when you can afford to step-up to a better one; this will become an excellent backup camera.

A reflector is also essential. It helps for the window shots and shots where the flashes are not really appreciated. Therefore, a reflector would serve the purpose for good photographs on those areas.

Beyond these few items, I think the only people who buy more gadgets than us photographers are golfers, and they have a bigger bag to carry their things in….

Chapter 3

Introduction to Professional Photography

A bride and groom's wedding day is probably one of the three biggest days in their lives, their wedding, buying their first home, and the birth of their first child, and it's your responsibly to make that wedding day one of the best they can have.

Talk about pressure? It's all on you that day, to record what's happening, to help them relive that day over and over. Keep in mind; She'll only wear that dress once (or we hope so anyway), the flowers wilt, the cake is eaten, the guests go home and for years to come all she'll have left from that day is her husband, her ring, and her sweetest **memories of the wedding.**

A recorded fact: at the times of disaster, *wedding pictures* are one of the *first* things to be saved. Remember, you are the one who is going to create these valuable photographs for them.

So much for the introduction to wedding photography, now let's get to the point of this book and that is to help you learn what pictures to take, when to take them and hopefully how to take them better.

Keep in mind; there is no **"perfect way"** to photograph a wedding, as much as they are all the same, each one of them is different and unique in their own way. The "**Flow Posing**" system is a way to make it easy on yourself because you will be working very hard over the next few hours and you need all the help you can get.

The suggestions I make are from personal experience of over thirty years, and hours and hours and days and days of studying with other professional wedding photographers.

I am now retired from actively photographing weddings but I am amazed at what poor quality I see being sold as "professional photography" now. Just because you buy a good camera and maybe a couple of lenses doesn't make you a professional.

Just because you take good "**snapshot pictures**" doesn't mean you're a "**Pro**".

You owe it to your client to do the best you can do, and if you do it well you can be rewarded with both money and personal pride in what you've done and created for the excited bride.

Now, let's get started on what you've bought this book for.

Chapter 4

Preplanning with the Bride

Y our first contact most likely will be by phone and your "bride to be" will want to know, "how much do you charge for a wedding?" and of course you can't answer that without knowing more about her special day; such as time of day, month and week, location, the number in the wedding party and so on.

So, try and convince her that she and maybe her mother needs to come to your office and see samples of your work and that you can better answer all her questions at that time. Offer or suggest that the groom should come and if all possible with his mother too.

Know for a fact that those mothers have a lot of control over what the bride will finally decide on. If she insists on a price tell her that your prices run from X to Z. State the very least you'll accept to give up your time to work for her on that day. Be careful not to under cut what you might get from another bride on that same day.

Explain you need to have a wedding consultation to get to know her, learn what she wants in pictures from that day and to convince her that you are the person that can best do all that for her.

Make it all about **her**, not you.

At the consultation you discuss her dress, her colors, and her bride's maids and how many, does she want a very "formal" wedding or a more casual one. Are photographs important to her or does she just want it "recorded" for posterity? The answer to that question will help you figure out what you will need to do for her.

I used a series of planning forms and "information for the Bride" when consulting with the bride and her family. See page 71 to access what my forms contained, and these forms can be modified for your business, by just adding your business name to the Word documents.

Once you learn all you can about her day, now is when you start telling her what you can do for her, and show examples of previous wedding images that you have taken.

Chapter 5

Samples of Past Work

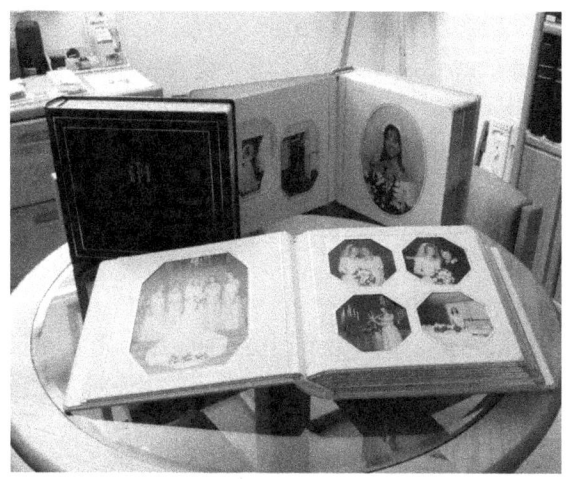

Make sure your *samples* are of top notch quality, <u>**now**</u> **isn't the time** to "explain that the prints are a little off color but her prints won't be, or that "these aren't what she'll get". Show her the best of you in your images.

Show a completed wedding that you have taken. I would often duplicate a brides order (second set of prints are cheaper) so I would have a complete wedding to show as a sample. Anyone can have several individual photos but to show a complete wedding gives her a better idea of what you can do.

Here's a "free idea" to give the "bride to be", that helps her on the wedding day (but really it's a bigger help for you: Suggest that she get some of the old carry-out-size brown paper bags, from her local grocery store, she then write on each one her attendants names, then takes them to the church on wedding day. When the girls start changing clothes, anything and everything that they take off including any jewelry, shoes, jeans and whatever, goes into their own personalized bags.

What a great idea, right? What that does for the girls is make it easy after the wedding to gather up their belongings to take to the reception if it's at a different location than the church, or to quickly clean out the bride's dressing room after ceremony. What it does for you is really ease the chore of "cleaning up the room when you come in to do pre-ceremony pictures". All you have to do now is to pick up and move paper bags rather than try to clean up a really messy dressing room. Gee, aren't you glad you thought of that! What an idea and you can give it to her for "free". What a nice guy you are.

Okay, you've succeeded in booking the wedding, be sure and have a "**Wedding Contract**" for her to fill out so you both have something in writing with all the important information, as to the when's and where's. Collect a deposit to lock in the date, day and time.

Without some commitment from her, you have no guarantee that you are for sure going to be her wedding photographer, and a deposit of say 50% of your finished price is that commitment. When you both sign the contract she has your commitment that you will be there for her as well.

I use a generic contract form I purchase from NEBS and you can find that online at http://www.nebs.com/nebsEcat/index.jsp and its item # 136.

After getting the contract, then you are sure about that you are hired. Now do one more thing that will really make things easier for you. Try to get as many names of the family members on both sides and try to remember most of them by heart, so that you can identify each of them by their name. Not only the bride and groom but most the party as well as the whole family are relying on you. It is a big day for the whole family. When you are asked to photograph the wedding ceremony, they put 100% of their trust with you. They have other things, a lot of things to think about that day. They do not want to think about photography after they have handed that job to you. It is your job after the contract is signed that you live up to their trust and try if you can do more.

Chapter 6

How to Ingratiate Your Professional Standing

O ffer to do engagement photos of her and her groom to be. You can do this either as part of the wedding package or as a separate portrait setting. This gives you a chance to meet him and get more comfortable with them both, and they with you. Ask them where they would like to have it taken, at a park, the place he proposed, or some "fun" place they like to go.

Be sure and have a clothing consultation to help them wear the right clothing. Avoid big patterns and try to have them in long sleeves; a bare arm isn't the most attractive thing to see in a photograph. Coordinated clothing helps make their faces the most obvious thing in the photograph. Joke with them and try and keep the mood light and fun for all of you. Be sure to get the photo of that engagement ring.

Even if it's just a chip, tell her how beautiful it is and that he certainly has good tastes in jewelry, and in his bride to be. Keep in mind that from now until after the wedding she's like Cinderella and on the way to the ball, and she'll undoubtedly tell her girl friends about her experiences of photographing with you, and if she brags you up big time, she just might be talking to your next bride.

Chapter 7

Day of the Ceremony

W hy Arrive at Least One Hour Early?

Now, getting on to the day of the wedding; I would hope I wouldn't have to mention this, but be sure and dress yourself either in a suit or at the very least a dark sport coat like a Navy Blazer and slacks. I always wore Navy Blazer and grey slacks, white shirt and tie. Have your shoes shined. Don't forget to have a handkerchief in your pocket; you're going to need it later.

All those things help establish you as a professional, not some jerk in jeans and tennis shoes looking like you know what you're doing. You want to fit into the overall picture, don't over dress the wedding party, but don't show up looking like a misfit slob.

 First impressions do make a difference and no telling what future bride might be looking for her photographer at this wedding too.

I always told my brides to have the wedding party dressed and ready for pictures an hour before ceremony, (knowing full well they wouldn't be, but when they were 30 minutes late it still gave me the 30 minutes that I needed to do the "before photographs", and I'll describe them shortly).

By you arriving at the church or place of ceremony an hour before, you have time to introduce yourself to the officiating person and ask what they do and do not allow during the ceremony.

Most officiating persons request **NO FLASH** during ceremony and that starts when the attendants enter the sanctuary. You normally **CAN** take a flash of the ring bearer and flower girl (if there is one), attendants and of course the Bride on entering.

I usually step back into a pew until time to step out into the aisle to take the picture and back into the pew to wait for the next subject. I tell the girls before hand what I'll be doing and tell them to keep coming and not to stop walking, do this with all the wedding party and by all means don't miss getting the bride and who ever is presenting her but let's get back to the pre ceremony photo's.

The Wedding Coordinator

You have introduced yourself to the officiating person, and by all means the wedding coordinator if there is one, (she can be your best help or your worst enemy depending on how you conduct your self in her church and at her wedding, even though it's not her wedding she treats it like it is). Now on to the bride and her attendants: Knock on the dressing room door and ask if they are dressed and if so go on in, no doubt the room will be a mess, (this is where those brown grocery sacks can be such a help to you), so quickly decide what you'll use for a background and start clearing the clutter out of the way.

Chapter 8

Pictures in the Bride's Dressing Room

I try to find space enough to allow a full length of the bride and for this one I don't worry about spreading the train, that photo will be done later.

A full length with her holding the bouquet, next step up for a nice Head and Shoulder image with the bouquet brought up close to the face, and a second one with a soft focus filter.

Have each girl step up with the bride, one at a time, for a nice head to waist image, have them get "cheek to cheek", even touching cheeks, always shoot two for protection in case of blinks, most of the time the bride will buy one of her with each of the girls and in some instances also purchase one for thank you gifts for each of her girls with her. (You can suggest that when she comes to view the previews).

If there is sufficient room, and you can back off far enough, try and get a group shot with the bride and all the girls including flower girl and ring bearer, go for it. That will sometimes sell too.

Ask the brides mother to now step up to the bride, a close head and shoulder of mom adjusting the veil and then one of them looking at the camera, step back and do a full length of the two, in most cases mom has a new dress for the wedding and you should have that recorded too, (doesn't hurt to compliment her on her choice of dresses).

Now have dad step up on the opposite side of the bride and do dad, bride, mom in a head and shoulder. Have dad and mom kiss her on the cheek at the same time, have mom step back and have the bride tilt her head onto dads shoulder and if it feels good to you, have her kiss him on the cheek.

Now dad drops down on one knee to put the garter on her leg. Have her point her toe to help ease getting it on, she pulls up the dress to a "modest" height and here's two photos.

Dad looking at the garter and then at her, if there's room in the room, have the attendants gather around the bride on both sides and do a quick group shot while dad is down on his knee.

Dad stands and can leave after a quick shot of mom and dad together, remember dad probably doesn't wear that tux very often and with mom and dad dressed up, it's another natural thing to do.

If there is a grandmother get her real quick with the bride and then get mom, bride, and grandma for a three generation group shot.

If the mother of the groom happens to be in the room, get her with the bride and then both mothers together with the bride, whew, still with me, all of this should take less than about 15 to 20 minutes.

It's called "**Flow Posing**" and by moving people in and out quickly it does flow and can be done in that time frame.

Ask the bride and the mom if there is anything else either of them would like before you go to photograph the men. Now is the time to reconfirm what you will be doing when they start down the aisle; you'll be stepping out in front of them for a photograph but they are to continue walking, you'll get out of their way after their photo.

If nothing else is wanted in the bride's room excuse yourself, and go to the grooms dressing area. This gives the girls time for a last minute touch up of makeup, or any other necessary things to take care of.

Chapter 9

Pictures in the Grooms Dressing Room

T he guys are easier, again quickly survey the room, pick out your background and start with the groom by himself. Add in the best man, head and shoulder of the two of them, ask the best man if he has the ring, ask him to show it to the groom holding it between thumb and forefinger, head and shoulder shot. Gather in the rest of the wedding party for a group. Now do them one at a time with the groom like you did the girls and the bride, (but a hand shake instead of cheek to cheek).

If you have the feelings that he would be up for a fun shot, pose the group with one of them showing him a watch (running out of time to leave), another with some fanned out money or credit cards acting like he's handing that over. The other guys can be wiping his brow (with your handkerchief because they won't have one) hanging onto his coat tail or fanning him, whatever fun idea you can come up with. If his mom and dad are there, by all means get them in a photo too. Whew, are you sweating yet?

Time to quickly go to the back of the church to get a photo or two of the guest book attendant, and check out the sanctuary to decide how far down the aisle you'll get in order to get the photos of the girls and bride entering. Select which pew, and sit down in it next to the aisle, (I always like to use the side on the girls right side, it makes it easier to step into the aisle for the photo and back into the pew with out having to turn yourself around). Anyway it was easier for me. You'll have to figure out what works best for you. Okay, catch your breath, the wedding is about to begin.

Chapter 10

Pictures of the Ceremony

T he music has started, the minister knows you'll abide by his wishes about no flash during ceremony, so when flash's do happen, and believe me they will, he'll know it wasn't you. When the mothers are ushered in, be sure to capture that moment. Try to remember to tell the dads to try and stay a little to the right of the usher so that their face shows in the photograph.

Get the grandparents too, if there are any, there and they haven't been pre-seated. Now, here comes the flower girl, step out of the pew, down to a knee to be close to the same height of the flower girl, pre-focus on a pew arm and when the girl gets to that pew "bam", you have your picture. Step back into the pew to wait for the ring bearer, same thing "bam" step back into the pew.

Now comes the attendants, remember you told them what you were going to do as far as stepping out in front of them. Pre-focused on that pew, smile at them and they'll smile back and "bam", step back out of their way.

Continue with all the attendants and now the big moment, everyone stands and "Here comes the Bride". Pre-focused on that pew, smile and she smiles back, she looks beautiful and dads beaming.

WOW, what a photograph, and you got it, step back into the aisle to let them pass. Once they have, step out and quickly grab a shot of the back of her dress and train with flash, and then immediately turn off your flash so you don't accidentally fire it off and upset the minister.

From now until the recessional you shoot nothing but time exposures; from the floor with the camera on a tripod (see http://acfs.biz/) to keep the image sharp, (since it'll be a slow exposure), with and without a star burst filter (sometimes called a cross star).

Quickly and quietly make your way to the balcony if there is one, and do wide angle, normal and telephoto images of the ceremony with and without the cross star filter. Move quietly because the attention should be on the wedding not on you, so move carefully and very silently without disturbing the ceremony. Back down to the floor and now you wait, if they use a kneeling bench that always makes a good image from the back of the sanctuary.

I should mention during this time, I never go down the center aisle and nor do I "creep" down the side aisles. This is a religious ceremony and I'm not there to interrupt it or to make a circus out of it by doing stupid things like that.

Back to the center of the aisle and now you wait. Wait for the minister to announce "I now present Mr. and Mrs. and you may kiss your bride".

Get that kiss shot and quickly turn your flash back on and wait for the recessional photos of the bride and groom, and if you're lucky and quick you might get more than one.

One of my favorites was the groom giving a "high-five" to a guest in a pew on the way out.

Chapter 11

Pictures after the Ceremony

Now you wait for the sanctuary to empty and the wedding party to return to the alter area. (This is why we should pay the wedding coordinator extra for helping get the wedding party and family back into the sanctuary.)

The ceremony is over and the fun is about to begin, but first you have to get all the formal photographs, the groups, the family groups, the wedding party, the bride and groom, and the bride full length with that beautiful train spread out behind her.

I have told or suggested to them, immediately after the ceremony and the recessional that the wedding party go to a "hidey hole" so the guests can be ushered out. (The wedding coordinator can be a big help with this.)

Okay, now stay with me, we're going to do "**Flow Posing**" again and get these photographs in approximately 20 minutes. It runs longer if the wedding party doesn't stay right there and family needed for photographs doesn't stay right there.

First photo, Bride and Groom with the minister or officiating person, this pleases them and allows them to get out of their robes if they are in one.

Now, the bride and groom with the entire wedding party including ushers. I personally still like to pose the girls on the bride's side and the guys on the groom's side, the bride and groom is the center of the group, for the big groups the train is behind the bride.

Start with the maid of honor and make the girls stand diagonally down the alter area and like wise with the best man and groomsmen. The ushers stand in back of the attendants.

Here is your posing tip: have the girls and the guys stand in a "models pose". That's ¾'s toward the bride and groom respectively, heel of the front foot pulls back into the arch of the rear foot.

This puts a nice curve to the human form, and prevents them from having their legs spread enough that you see thru between them. The girls of course are holding their bouquets so they have something to do with their hands. Have the men drop their hands to their sides so they aren't standing in a "fig leaf" pose with their crossed hands covering their crotch.

I guarantee their hands will light up the photograph if you leave them in front. They stand out "white" against the dark tux or suit pants and that's a "no-no". On buttoning their jackets, it's really personal choice as long as they all do the same thing, buttoned looks neater if they don't have vests; with vests it really makes no difference to me. If they are just in suits and not tuxes, by all means they should be buttoned, add the flower girl and ring bearer in front of the bride and groom.

Take two quick shots, now the ushers are pulled out, two quick shots with the wedding party. Now pull out the little kids, two quick shots, and pull out all the attendants except maid of honor and best man.

As people are pulled out, ask them not to leave as you will need them for additional photos shortly.

Now you're down to bride and groom, turn them ¾ to each other, his right hand into the small of her back, make sure his fingers don't "creep out from behind her", his left hand moves up under the bouquet, "to help her since she shaking so bad", usually always gets a laugh from the observers. Bring the train around to front and spread it out to show it off, sometimes the maid of honor will help do that.

Two quick full length with them looking at camera, two looking at each other, have him kiss her again, step up for a head and shoulder shot, both regular and soft focus. Ask him to step out to the side, now do her head and shoulder with and without soft focus filter, then step back for a full length.

Ask the groom to step back in on the bride's right side and ask his parents to step up on the brides left side, mother next to the bride; be sure dad's coat is buttoned. Crowd them in nice and close, two shots, mom and dad shifts enough to allow the groom to come back to the brides left side and her mom and dad step up on her right side.

You now have brides parents, bride and groom, grooms parents in a group, two quick shots, ask the grooms parents to step out and two quick shots of brides mom and dad with bride and groom. Now what you have is a photo of both sets of parents with bride and groom, which is the photo they'll buy, you have bride and groom with his parents this pictures they'll buy, and bride and groom with her parents, which they'll buy.

You just sold three photos instead of one, pretty slick huh? If lucky enough to have grandparents there, they can be added in when doing each families side.

Now quickly ask for all the girls to come back up for a formal shot with the bride, two quick shots, time for a fun one if they want it, step the girls out and ask for the guys to join the bride on both sides. Two quick shots, now ask the two closest to the bride to lean in and kiss her on the cheeks, fun shot and she likes that.

Now let the bride step out and rest for a minute, add in the groom with the grooms men, two quick shots, let the men step out and add the girls back in again on both sides, two quick shots and ask the two closest to kiss him on the cheek like the guys did with the bride.

Depending on the bride and groom, I'll sometimes stand the bride just into camera range on the side and have her turn to the crowd and put her hands on her hips as if she were upset with the girls "kissing her man". It's a fun shot that helps people kind of forget how long it's taking.

Bride and groom back to the center of the alter area, and now you can do any and all family groupings that either or both family's want. As you finish the groups with attendants, they can leave the sanctuary and go ahead to the reception area (if they are not needed for family groups).

Letting those people in the reception area know the bride and groom will soon be arriving.

As they all leave and you're down to the bride and groom, this is when you do your romantic shots of them close together. Some soft focuses, gentle kisses and have them hold the lighting candles over the flame of the Unity candle, her on your left and him on the right.

She holds her candle in her left hand and their two front hands hold each other with the lighting candles making the flame of the Unity candle flare up, with and without a cross star filter, both regular and soft focus.

A special image I think I created, and always try to do, have the groom move down to a pew, left hand side of the aisle, step into the pew facing the entrance of the sanctuary, he sits on the back of a pew, puts his feet on the seat of the pew in front of him, crosses his arms with the left hand on top of his right arm (showing his new ring). The bride puts her bouquet in his lap so his crotch is covered, she then slides in close to him, standing, her right hand on his back, her left hand (with her new rings) softly on his shoulder by his flower and she leans in toward his head, shoot it tight (do not lower than the flowers in his lap). Do it with and with out soft focus.

Break the pose, he turns and sits in the pew where he had his feet, she joins him on his right side. Spread her dress over his pants. The bridal bouquet lies on their lap, his right hand is lowered over the flowers, and her hand goes on top of his at an angle with her thumb sliding under his hand.

Gently spread their fingers ever so slightly so that both the rings show and two quick shots very tight on the hands and flowers. While you're taking this shot be sure and ask them to smile. Of course their faces aren't showing, so it's kind of a "joke" to relax them some.

With a wedding party of four to six and a reasonable amount of "family groupings", you have just photographed the wedding formal photographs in approximately 20 to 30 minutes. Since you already told the bride and her mother about how long it would take, and it has, you're still in good graces with both mom and bride. But do not forget to ask the bride and/or the groom if they would like any photographs to be taken outside, in some places they would love to be photographed at with their wedding dresses on, like their first proposal place or dating place, or somewhere they loved to visit frequently or would they like to be photographed somewhere of your choice. If they have their own priority place of choice then you should try to visit there before the wedding day. This is because you can be sure of the lighting, backgrounds and angles to take the photographs from, so that you can take perfect photographs.

If they want to go to a place of your choice then well and fine, as you would already know the details of those places. Be sure this has been discussed before the wedding and that time has been scheduled for it, so you don't over extend the time between formal groups and the reception.

Chapter 12

The Reception

N ow on to the reception, are you still with me, sweating yet? Whew, didn't think you could do it did you? But with the "**Flow Posing**", it really does move pretty smoothly and pretty quickly, and with practice it gets even better.

At the reception, the very first photo I take is of the cake. I do that while they are setting up their reception line, if they have one. Some brides have chosen to do away with this old tradition, and in that case I try to get them to do the cake cutting and bouquet tossing first thing.

Guests just don't hang around receptions like they used to. We as people have gotten too busy and don't have the time to just "hang around", therefore, they get their cake and leave. So let's get the cake cutting out of the way first thing.

Another tip for the reception photography is that you should visit the reception area at least once before the wedding day. This will give you an idea where to move, how to move, and just plan out where you would set up your tripod and also all your equipment, so that every corner in there gets known to you, and you can easily accommodate yourself there with your equipment easily at the reception time.

The Cake

Position the bride and groom behind the cake table, normally the "cutting knife" is a blade about an inch wide and usually about 10 to 12 inches long. Have the groom on the bride's side between here and the cake. The reason for this is you want the white of the cake separated from the white of the bride's dress by the darkness of the tux or suit of the groom.

She holds the knife in her right hand; his left hand is in the small of her back and his right on top of her hand. For picture purposes have them hold the knife at about the middle layer of the cake, two pictures, one looking at the cake and one looking at the camera.

To actually cut a piece to feed each other with, move the knife to the bottom layer, make a cut straight down the lower layer of the cake, move the knife over approximately an inch, cut straight down again. Now turn the knife point down between those cuts, push it straight down, and "rake" out the piece on a plate or napkin, cut that piece in half and you have your feeding pieces.

I suggest for pictures that they do not smash the cake into each others faces, but if that's what they want to do, get the picture. If they agree not to, have the groom use his back hand, (most distant from the camera) to feed his bride, if he uses his right hand, he covers up to much of her face, and she can use her right hand to feed him. Best photos happen if they feed one at a time.

The Toast

It's time for the toasting: Fill their glasses about half full, I have a series of three photos I like to take here, with the cake still in the side of the photo, have the groom hold his glass in his right hand. The bride holds hers in her left hand. Have them face each other, extend their arms straight out toward the camera. Lower them, so you can see their faces and touch the glasses to a toast. Focus on the glasses throwing bride and groom slightly out of focus. Second shot is the same pose but focus on them, looking at each other and the glasses out of focus. The third is when they then "wrap arms" and drink at the same time.

Bouquet Toss

Place a chair in the middle of the dance floor, if there is one or the middle of the room if there isn't. Find another one to stand on so you can have some altitude to see over the bride when she throws the bouquet. Have all the single girls gather on the edge of the area.

If there is a D. J. have him do the count down. I like to have the bride "practice" once before she actually throws it, and when she does actually throw it, try to catch it in midair. She'll be facing you throwing over her shoulder, and the girls will be hopefully trying to catch it.

You only really get one chance for this one and it takes practice to catch it at the midair, and even then you don't always get it. But be prepared for an action shot, if there is any action among the girls.

The Garter

Now the grooms turn, sometimes the D.J. will have something special or fun for him to do, and if so, let him run with it and be prepared to record what ever happens. If not, you're in control, have the single men line up where the girls had been, turn the chair to face them, ask the bride to have a seat, the groom down on a knee, he'll either reach up under the dress or she may, depending on style of dress, pull up the skirt to show the garter (usually right above the knee).

Let the groom remove it and be prepared for who knows what. He may simply slide it down her leg or may end up taking it off with his teeth, just be ready for what ever. Once it's off, have him stand either behind or beside his bride, and "shoot" the garter towards the men and try again to catch it in midair. This one is a little tougher since it's smaller and doesn't have the color the bouquet does.

A cute picture to get after all that, if the persons catching the items happen to be friends or at least not little kids, is to get the garter on the sleeve of the guy and the girl who caught the bouquet together with the bride and groom for a quick group photo.

Still holding up? You're almost done; ask the bride and groom if they are changing clothes before they depart or if they are leaving in formal clothes and when they plan on leaving.

Chapter 13

The Dance or Departure

I f there is a dance, be sure and get that first dance with bride and father, groom and mother and bride and groom together. If there is to be a dance and you don't want to hang around for that (and sometimes they can go on for hours).

I suggest taking the bride and groom to the car and "posing up" their "going away" photos. If they agree, slip out and see if the car is decorated and if so, be sure and get some images of that, better yet if they're still doing the deed capture some of the culprits in action for the fun of it.

In any case, have the bride and groom get into the car, front seat if they're driving them selves away or back seat if someone else is driving, roll down the window, have them slide close together and frame them in the window opening. If leaving in a limo, get them standing by the back door, let them get into the limo, ask the driver if you can get in the front seat and shoot back towards them in the rear seat. Most of the times they'll agree but always ask first.

Now, if they are actually leaving at this time, guests will line up outside the door the bride and groom will exit out of, with their rice bags (usually bird seed now, rice gets eaten by birds and I guess they can't digest it and causes them to die so you can suggest the bird seed at the original consultation as a conservation suggestion).

Position yourself by the car and as the couple exit the reception area and are engulfed by thrown rice or bird seed or balloons or bubbles or whatever. Be sure and capture that photo too.

Chapter 14

The Finish

Okay, whew, you think you're done? One more courtesy to do is to ask both mothers if there are any other photo's they'd like before you depart. If so, take them and if not, collect your gear, make your way to your car, stow the stuff in the trunk and loosen up that tie and think to yourself; "Wow, I did it, just like he said I would, and I feel tired but proud of what I've just accomplished."

Now, let them enjoy their guests, eat if they are having a dinner and you can do a few candid shots around the room. Most likely they're not going to buy many of them anyway and take advantage of a few minutes to get a glass of water, you deserve it.

I should mention at this time I never, repeat never, take a piece of cake or go thru a serving line if they are having a dinner unless specifically invited to by either the parents or the bride and groom. And I absolutely NEVER have an alcoholic drink until I have taken my last photograph, put the camera away, and am again invited to by parents or bride and groom to do so. If a guest sees you "drinking" on the job, or if for some reason some of the photographs should happen to not turn out, I guarantee you it'll be your fault because you were drinking and most likely "drunk" and that's why they didn't turn out.

Now once the camera is put away and if I'm invited, I'll certainly enjoy no more than two drinks because I was invited to. At that point, I feel if invited and I refused it would be rude and an insult to those inviting me to partake.

Chapter 15

The Wrap Up

Practicing your Poses

L et me mention that I know all this is coming at you pretty fast, I would suggest that you use your wife or girl friend or whoever, as a "stand in bride", and walk your self through all these poses at home, in your mind.

Practice and be sure you understand what you're trying to do with the "**Flow Posing**". Don't wait until you're actually at a wedding to "practice them". That would be very unfair to both you and your bride, and would certainly make you look very "unprofessional". Not the image you want to project.

Finding a Good Lab

Now, depending on how you choose to present your previews of the wedding and reception, be sure and have a good relationship with your lab, who will print your final images for the couple and family pictures.

There are many good ones out there. I personally have used Miller's Professional Imaging in Pittsburg Kansas (information on http://www.millerslab.com) and I feel they are the best there is. I have used them for over thirty years and they can help make you look like the best. And, if there happens to be a problem, most likely they can help there too, providing there is something to work with.

Albums, you're on your own there, there are so many options there you'll just have to find your own way along that path. Also, do remember another thing, these days people are into DVD or drives. Make up a slideshow with beautiful touchy music at the background, and with most lovely pictures you find attractive, and make the slide-show covering most the wedding, funny moments and some sensitive moments added. I can bet that some of the family members are going to so love it that it may bring tears into their eyes.

Professional Photographers

As a side note, let me strongly recommend that you check into and consider joining local professional photography associations, and at the state level and even the national Professional Photographers of America. They all have meetings, and seminars and conventions that you can attend, classes you can take, and you'd be amazed at what you learn and pick up just by associating with the kind of people you want to become.

Special Forms Needed for Professional Weddings

Find copies of information that I used to give to my prospective brides, to not only hopefully help them to select me as their photographer but also to help them make good decisions on their "special day". **Bonus**: **download your form pack go to http://acfs.biz/forms.html**. Feel free to redesign any or all of them, use them or not, it's your choice.

As a final thought, keep in mind you won't book every bride you talk to, **but most important of all, don't "give" your work away.** You work hard to learn your trade, you should be attending seminars and meetings with other photographers to talk and learn about new equipment, and new ways of doing things and you should be paid for that investment in knowledge.

That's what the bride and groom are paying for, not a bunch of 8 X 10 pieces of paper, but your knowledge and time it takes to capture the memories that go on those pieces of paper. There will always be someone out there charging more than you do and someone out there undercutting everyone; charge fairly and deliver what you charge for.

Be proud of what you produce and you can make a living being a "Wedding Photographer".

With these skills and using the "Flow Posing System" that I have presented in this book, you now have all the necessary tools to succeed in this business; the rest is up to you.

God Bless and good luck.

Johnie L Cook

Other Titles You May Enjoy

- Wedding Disasters
  For more information, visit:
  amazon.com/dp/B007GNIEZW

- How to buy Cheap Tickets
  For more information, visit:
  amazon.com/dp/B0075ODUEC

- How to make Good Photos
  For more information, visit:
  amazon.com/dp/B006QDBUF4

- Travel Planner Guide and Software
  For more information, visit:
  amazon.com/dp/B007DKQ6SA

- Planning your Trip
  For more information, please visit
  amazon.com/dp/B007DMX0NC

Attention Writers:

Econohost Publishing can publish your Books

http://econohost.info

Email: richard@econohost.info